T0194819

LIGHT ON
HATHA YOGA

WILLIAM DUPREY

BALBOA.PRESS
A DIVISION OF HAY HOUSE

Balboa Press books may be ordered through booksellers or by contacting:

Balboa Press
A Division of Hay House
1663 Liberty Drive
Bloomington, IN 47403
www.balboapress.com
844-682-1282

Print information available on the last page.

ISBN: 979-8-7652-4268-1 (sc)
ISBN: 979-8-7652-4267-4 (hc)
ISBN: 979-8-7652-4269-8 (e)

Library of Congress Control Number: 2023909833

Balboa Press rev. date: 06/21/2023

Dedication

Mela, the first of her kind.

Ita, for all that I have forgotten.

Family and friends, thank you, always.

Gurus and students, may this light be yours.

Special thanks

Princess Diana and Lulu David Brenner for your amazing edits and insight.

Table of Contents

1. Introduction from Sarah Ruhl

William Duprey was my teacher for three years when I lived in California. He taught me yoga and meditation. Sometimes I went to his classes, sometimes we met individually, as is common in classical yoga. He gave me Patanjali's yoga sutras and I studied them. Eventually I got married and got pregnant. "You will be a householder now," said Will. At the time, I didn't understand the full implications of that sentiment.

I moved from California to New York with my burgeoning family. I took some classes with Dharma Mittra, Will's teacher, but the classes were quite physically demanding, and I found that after I gave birth, I didn't feel strong enough for such intense asanas. In New York, I got very busy with my writing and with my family, and I could never find another teacher quite like Will. So I stopped practicing yoga. What a terrible lesson! Should the yoga not have stayed in me?

Perhaps it stayed in me in a different form. I continued to write, and I embarked on a study of Buddhism. There is a text in Tibetan Buddhism called "Words of my Perfect Teacher." Part of the concept of the book is that the more you think of your teacher as perfect, the more perfections you will receive. There is a paradox here--an acknowledgment that no one is perfect, but if we *imagine* our teacher's perfection, and allow ourselves to give the teacher devotion, we receive more wisdom from the teacher. One thing I always loved about Will's teaching is that he always acknowledged his own imperfections, his human-ness, with humor and humility. I think there is something moving and miraculous (now that I am a teacher of writing) in a teacher trying her or his best to teach, knowing full well that she is vulnerable, that she suffers, that she doesn't have perfect wisdom. Still, we teach.

Recently I reconnected with Will, my teacher. He let me read his extraordinary new work *Light on Hatha Yoga,* which is a revelatory translation of classical yoga text with his own unique commentary that helps the reader find our own way into this ancient wisdom. I was so grateful for this book's teachings. At first I read it quickly, as though terribly thirsty for water. I will keep this book with me, and read it many times slowly. The text reminded me that "Dying can be something, anything that stops us from fully living." It reminded me of what I have been missing, being away from the practice. For example, this line struck me mightily in the present moment:

"How can we see the world if we do not peer into it - the nature of existence. The mind becomes occupied with location: country, state, political party. I cannot know the sky if I never look at or care over which location it resides. It is above me but not beyond my reach."

How true this is. And what wonderful medicine for the times we are living in. The following text you are about to read is quite literally *medicine*, reminding us that part of karma yoga is "doing without desire of reward." It's easy to feel in this country that you are surrounded by yoga practitioners who want the sexy yoga pants without the meditation, or the sculpted abs without the breathing practice, or who want the fruits of meditation without the dharma, the spiritual teachings behind the practice. William Duprey, even when he was quite young, shared classical yoga teachings with his students. He wasn't inventing new terms for poses like: "rocket dog"; instead, he was going back to the classical terminology and seeing what he could uncover for the contemporary practitioner.

Sometimes it feels like yoga is being co-opted by the forces of capitalism in the west, and occasionally the forces of right wing ideology in the east. But in this fresh, free, poetic and accessible translation, classical yoga is waiting for you without any imposition. William Duprey indeed shines a light on the text, giving us the gift of quiet illumination. Whether you have studied with him and want him by your side in the form of a book, or you've never studied with him and want to gain insight from him, this book can be your guide to a new relationship with the concept and practice of yoga.

Duprey writes here: "Yoga is an ideology of habit." Then he goes on to compare yoga to a beautiful ancient rug that gets more luminous with use. Indeed! May your rug be beautiful and be walked upon! May you sit and practice with this text with no thought of reward. May this lineage help you and be your guide.

Introduction

The ordinary is so magical, present and simple that it is often not worth talking about. Not because the ordinary lacks worth, but because the words used to describe the ordinary, even the word ordinary itself, falls short of the experience.

Imagine thousands, millions of lines or threads woven together. These chords stretch beyond the physical you and throughout the universe and beyond. This fabric of highways includes the energetic body and mind energy, as well as all the energy around the body and mind. These systems go into influencing biophysical function and subtle level healing solutions within our most expansive states of consciousness.

Sanskrit, the language associated with the historical origins of yoga, is an active language. All the sounds that make up the alphabet reside within and stimulate the larger chakras in your energetic system. This system stretches out with innumerable lines that stretch through you and the universe. To contemplate the ancient texts of yoga is to engage in this system.

The Hatha Yoga Pradipika is one of the most influential texts within the study of Hatha Vidya (knowledge through physical control) and Raja Yoga (control of the mind in order to enter the mental state of yoga). If we look at the essence of the Hatha Yoga Pradipika, its contribution as a written body of material offers very particular and precise practices which aim for Hatha Vidya and the attainment of Raja Yoga. Outside of the casually vague instructions "sit on asana" or "do asana," most yogic texts did not specify which poses to practice or how to practice them. This you learned from a teacher. The Pradipika actually list a specific amount of postures to practice: eleven preliminary postures and the four contemplative ones.

For reasons I hope to illuminate in the following pages, I have translated the Pradipika in poetic form through a process of steady practice of the aforementioned postures followed by observation. After practicing morning rituals, I would sit with a passage or two and translate the experience, as opposed to the manual description. I started with the chapter on Asana not because it was for gaining steadiness, but because it was about sensation. Sensation gives you experience and awareness of

WILLIAM DUPREY

existence. It is in that existence that true awareness can come into our lives.

As you gain more knowledge of yoga and the depth of the subtle systems, you can look at the text and expand upon balancing deeper introspection and the state of yoga as found in Raja Yoga. In essence, going within the practices, in the way the practices are orchestrated, creates a mechanism for the experience of yoga. I refer to this process as a delayed mechanism.

*

I became interested with this text at the suggestion of my guru. Originally, my questions were on specific gains (health, healing, etc.), but as the process continued, it revealed something much more interesting in a specific path or structure to yoga. This is where I really became excited about this text and the surrounding schools of thought. By school of thought, I am not referring to a style of yoga nor a particular lineage, though lineages tend to pass on particular philosophical dispositions, nor do I mean a relationship with a particular deity or a founding principle philosophy (i.e. sankhya, yyaya, yoga, etc.). What

I am referring to is the measurement in which we use the technique, in this case Hatha Yoga, and all the tools that make up Hatha Yoga (i.e. asana, bandha, pranayama, mudra, kriya, mantra) as well as the way in which they are positioned to create a controlled mechanism for peak experience.

The peak experience in the practice of yoga, even yoga contained of physical manipulation, is the culmination of prana in a collective process of consciousness as one sets out on a regular practice to understand truth. Similarly, the mind that flutters to understand truth prods different intonations of the mind to see something more clearly. When it arrives at the result, the thought pattern becomes still, settled and one truth is obtained. As with the mind, so the body, breath and energies of those systems can be directed; in turn, they influence the mind (Raja Yoga). If I let the mind run wild at full force, it will tire quickly or be unable to tame. If I direct it slowly toward a goal, it will gain steadiness and avoid distraction. In time, ease will result. Ease brings about the blossoming of contentment and the peak experience. And this is what I became very fascinated with: How is the peak experience directed by these techniques?

*

WILLIAM DUPREY

Searching for the peak experience, one can get hung up on details, or confused by them. Researching many websites, texts and scriptural references, I compared notes on how to practice the eleven postures described in the Pradipika. Some are quite confusing. There was not a common consensus on what the poses actually looked like.

As part of the process of discovering the peak experience, I tested the postures over a fifteen-year period. It was important for me to allow the asana to have its own affect. I did not perform the postures searching for what it was supposed to do according to texts or interpretation of texts. Instead, I relied on what was actually felt and experienced to inform my understanding. This was not an extremely complicated process, but it required faith in the experience itself, as well as a lot of space or observation time. Trying to keep your head straight while sifting though information and theory in and surrounding a yogic text can be arduous. My aim in translating the Pradipika was to focus on something base and felt, the peak experience, without engaging in a deeply tangled philosophical debate.

*

During this time of deep study and practice, I was actively reading, and thereby greatly influenced by, a lot of Tamil and Siddha poetry. Although I am aware of the potential loss that can occur in interpretation, there is also the potential for clarity, insight and creativity. Much like poetry itself, interpretation can move us from what we know of one word or concept and forever change that universe of understanding. The very transmutation that comes about into poetic interpretation is hopefully represented in this version of the Pradipika.

In this instance, poetry represents codified instruction, sometimes relating to practices, techniques and thought. Deciphering it can take time, as a lot of the understanding is through knowledge from experience. In this case, a technique and an outcome may be revealed, and very few can understand the experience only in the mind as thought which carries us into the state of samadhi. There are no real short cuts, and though the authors of these bodies of works are writing at times the instruction to the state, the method in which I used was borrowed from writing while in a state and instead of writing a technique to the state; the attempt was to expand the state.

When you look at your favorite translation or directly at the passage of the Hatha Yoga Pradipika, you will see that the lines match up with standard translations — meaning that 1.1 in the translation matches line 1 of the first chapter of the Pradipika also 1.1. This translation is not direct; it is an interpretation of a conceived experience of what the passage could become — a state of understanding. Therefore, at times you will notice an extra number appear (i.e. 1.1.1.) which indicates an alternative or additional interpretation to 1.1 in the original text. I have also categorized parts of the text into single passages so you might see a grouping such as 1.1-1.4 which indicates lines 1.1 through 1.4 are brought into one interpretation. In this regard, if you would like to compare, it is very helpful to have a copy of the Pradipika with you. If not, I believe you will equally enjoy the contemplations alone.

Now let's begin!

Acknowledgements

All of the quoted practices that start each chapter are from Pancham Singh. Along side this most notable translation, I am very thankful for the translation of Dr. M. A. Jayashree.

Her devotional work with Sanskrit, alongside Professor M. A. Narasimhan, knows no measure. I would also like to thank recent translations by Swami Muktibodhananda and stunning, most recent translation by Brian Dana Akers. These translations were a boon in comparing to Singh's translation and when used in orchestrated translation thought into poetic experience of my own practices. Thank you!

2. Light on Hatha Yoga

A poetic interpretation and contemplation of the Hatha Yoga Pradipika: First Pada - Form

1.1 - It is You, the first one. Arising of stillness. The steps of knowledge you have taken created the first path. The one that is complete. Your way is completed.

I desire to be complete and will follow this path truly and with knowledge of You. Please expel distraction from my mind and body to see You continuously and clearly.

1.1.1 - Your name travels with such joy, hearing a parent and child participate in joy itself, of full potential. It comes in many names, forms, but is born of You and I desire it for me.

1.2 - Salutations to You, My Dear One. Like a lover, I hold you in my breath, that the life in me forms the sound praises of your way, knowledge and a sound position. My breath rises from you and so does the spirit of me and all that is within.

1.3 - Wandering, lost to darkness, from energies perceived within or without, there is a desire in that wandering. A desire to know thy self and soul as you embody. Show me steadiness and light.

1.4 - As you have learned by the grace of others, there is faith for me from the compassion of the masters before you and in your compassion now.

1.5 - 1.9 - If I call upon you by name or essence, this call existed before me and will be after it is said – Mahasiddhas break the bonds of time, roaming the universe freely when called upon.

1.5 - 1.9.0 - The many ways in which sun illuminates the world; it does not ask to be called.

1.10 - Even nature - like the sun - knows only its own natural way. There is not an ill intent yet we protect ourself from its unlimited power, redirect the energy and space for it. Here it becomes a support system - we feel its uplifting way - its natural way becomes us.

the first sentence confuses the metaphor a bit. let it ride from 1.9.0:

The sun bears no ill intent, yet we must protect ourselves from its unlimited power, redirecting the energy and space for it. It becomes a support system when we feel its uplifting way, when its natural way becomes us.

I resonate with the expansion from the sun to all of nature. I also didn't read it as a metaphor but as truth. And protecting ourself from all of nature is very different that protecting oneself from the sun.

1.10.1 - I drop into your shade - I know not the sun - the way you love so fully - protect me, shelter me, uplift me into my own natural way.

1.11 - You have revealed a way within me. From you, I have become. Your becoming is not me. My becoming is supported by you. When I have revealed myself, I shall show this light.

1.11.1 - All that is within has come from you. I have absorbed these ways. Only the essence is revealed. The way cannot be given to all. Unique are the ways of all beings and teachings.

1.12 - A sound place is required for cultivating inner awareness. Freedom comes in specifics, needs to be met, advancements that inhibit growth.

WILLIAM DUPREY

1.13 - There are particulars which I should prepare. These have been prepared before and allow me freedom and some control of that which is without. I will go within with steadiness, free of obstacles.

1.14 - Knowing steadiness attracts all things to me, pleasures and pains alike. Freeing myself from anxiety, I only wish to attract the light I see within my guru and in the guru I see light everywhere. This is not a separation from darkness, but an exploration to seek light and familiarity in all aspects of the higher self. In the manner instructed by a teacher, I must sit and be steady before anything of substance is revealed, for only in steadiness, free from distraction, can I find what it is distracting and what I distract myself with.

1.15 - Being a steady state of mind, yoga can be discontinued by excess. Similarly, by the same rules, the fluctuation of the mind can be made too firm with rules. Keeping company with those who are not of the same mind allows for distraction. Over eating, the inability to digest physically or mentally, and talkativeness can create rumination and lead to imaginary systems by which to live. These are some examples in how the state of yoga can be faltered. Many exist already for the route to steadiness has been limited due to modernity.

1.16 - Yoga — belonging to many things with nothing belonging to it — can be brought about with steadiness and success when one looks deeper into the recipient or true self.

There are ways in which we can test the self through knowledge based on testing, courage to take upon this task, exploring an inner connection of company, daring, perseverance, and faith that we are always headed toward union, success and realization.

I like the grammar edit of "—" in the first sentence. Instead of "test the self through knowledge based on testing", perhaps:

~test the self through knowledge gained by practices

~steady the self through knowledge gained through testing

…?

1.17 - The rules of conduct are plenty. They should not be rules we fail to live by but rather something that uplifts the moral being and the way we move in the world. The rules of conduct should be greatly tested to continue to evolve our being to the maximum harmonic value possible.

1.18 - Observation alone is an amazing measurement. Many will falter on the path of yoga from observation alone. Restraining energy to bring about an inner radiance follows these observations. They are listed as rules rather than qualities of the spirit through the faculties in which we participate in culture and the human experience.

1.19 - Asana pertaining to the body, which alone has freedoms and obstacles, is tended to first with regularity to gain a steady posture in living, health in living energy experiences, and lightness in living attitude. All of this living is experienced first in the body with a seat or position which is adapted in living.

1.20 - Certain asanas are grand and noticeable while others are internal and Self seeking-- all categories lead to a source knowledge in the physical first. Amongst these are certain poses of particular interest to Munis, who not only experience energetic qualities in the physical form but shape them.

1.21–1.36 - We sit in the positions of life — a delayed mechanism of involution.

1.37 - 1.38 - Amongst all things are gems, jewels and pearls - something so ordinary yet completely magnificent in its own nature. As even amongst all asana, there are a few gems which yield an elevated experience to the keen observer.

(N.B. or author's note on asana: edits (As it moves one from application to absorption, the methodology becomes steady to reveal a non-technique. It is my desire to talk more about this, but even through the practices of postures, I have run into a limitation in teaching. I am not limited in teaching where the posture goes, but in teaching how the posture can extend forever. By this, I do not mean to make the posture second nature; nor am I speaking in terms of muscle systems, alignment systems or energetic patterns. The seat alone can become the seat alone. Through the structure is the unbound. This can be something simple, rather than a physical goal that is so often sought after... one is lead to an experience in the physical that is connected though and beyond the mind rather than to the mind).

1.39 - 1.40 - Amongst jewels, names are common. There are names that categorize a collective. Amongst the collective, there are those that are flawless-- perfect in mind, energy and form. The form may not be ideal and the mind far from your reach, full of energy you cannot harness. There are postures amongst postures, practices and yields as desired that bring together all energies within and without.

1.41 - 1.42 - The way is one. If any paths flowing into one terminate at different points, they still end as one, start as one, and are the one not subject to time. When we see all things in a line of equal length, as points along a flat surface, this is progression, delineation and stillness. The infinite mountains become smooth plains with millions of years between them spent in a single breath. The moment when you let your hand go from taking another, teemed with positions of life enraptured in a charka of numbers that repeats itself. Within your heart is the same beat. Your mind makes it wait. The power within you is contained within the thought: the heart's beating as a whisper in a crowd.

1.43 - Siddhasana alone should one practice. Alone one should practice, even within a room of many others. The hearts of the wind are calm and held without tension in a moment of true content. Nourishment and time begin to dance so delicately; awareness arrives through contemplation. The self can arise.

1.44 - Completion from one creates a oneness in all; success in one alone draws all near and to the source of the limitless.

WILLIAM DUPREY

1.45 - That which is bound, including a technique, yields one unlike another. The technique becomes receptivity as clarity and perfection follows.

1.46 - 1.51 - Padmasana. Death shall befall you at time appropriate. One is pulled from the direction of death, from misbalances and suffering. Concentrate at the tip of the nose like staring into a river with landscape, with excitement in looking at something beautiful, let your tongue slide to the upper palate as you slide the lower palate to the chest. Take that which flows down the legs upward. This can be done by those with intelligence in the body. Form that intelligence in the navel where the river of air that flows south heads north by used of the great gate and meets the northern river now flowing south from the jalandhara bandha. All life comes to me. Within my mountainous stability is a steady flow of intelligence and guided power. Delight beyond measure. Breath bound by none.

WILLIAM DUPREY

1.52 - 1.54 - Simhasana - some things are sacred beyond measure. They are adored and absorbed in the formless.

.

1.55 - 1.59 - Bhadrasana, Goraksasana - A home is kept with a heart. A pure heart is clear and distinct; it pulls even the unsteady to it. Nothing can tamper with it, even while fingers draw circles in water. Even the water wishes it was full of delight. A sound is heard by others but even the heart is beyond vibration.

1.60 - What is this self that I fill? Is it something to satiate beyond survival and general well-being? Should I not provide a fullness from the warmth of food cooked properly and sweetened to match wellness and disposition? Should I not be purified in my offering to the grandness outside of myself? Some remains always for Siva, some for me and some room for change as sustenance, spirit and form come together.

1.61 - 1.64 - Steadiness needs fuel. The fire should burn proper. If I light it ablaze, I have no room for longevity or transmutation. The process delayed leaves an undesirable fullness; dampness results. If I do not tend to it, I know not the benefits. In stillness I seek inner fire amongst self-awareness and personal doctrine — the elixir of living undisturbed.

1.65 - 1.66 - Inactivity is lifeless. Life leaves the body of young, old, too old, lean or other when not rejuvenated. Sip, bathe and drench the body according to your desire of fullness. Success is establish when desire meets intelligence and living.

1.67 - How can we see the world if we do not peer into it — the nature of existence? The mind becomes occupied with location: country, state, political party... I cannot know the sky if I never look at or care over in which location it resides. It is above me but not beyond my reach. Tending to it, I begin to know its ways. Through the action, our ways are one, our knowledge is equal and inseparable.

1.68 - Falling leads to looking up. Success from practice. Practice embraces moments of failure strung along the breath. Dress should provide comfort and adoration for what is to come. What is to come has not occurred and is best left unmentioned.

1.69 - Yoga is unnamed, a method of forming a position in living.

WILLIAM DUPREY

3. Sri Adinatha

The first passage in the Hatha Yoga Pradipika often reads translated as, "Salutation to Adinatha who expounded the knowledge of Hatha Yoga, which like a staircase leads the aspirant to the peaks of Raja Yoga."

The emphasis or salutation to Adinatha makes up the framework in this process of practice. If we look at the words individually, this will help not only on the process but what the process is. I do have to add that, when this passage is recited in Sanskrit, the word "Sri" is often placed in front of Adinatha. Sometime you also do find that, in English, the author will use Sri Adinatha or omit this name altogether and simple use Shiva.

Sri can be interpreted as the ability to manipulate shakti. Shakti is the divine energy within all of us. Sometimes shakti is referred to as feminine, a serpent or snake of kundalini, or kundalini rising. In this regard, I personally see shakti as a completion rather than an attainment — an accomplishment indicating the power of perfection, that one has realized their co-creative source energy. The spark within is a reflection. This goes beyond techniques to illustrate points of the teachings which are applicable to those practicing the physical and mind related practices of yoga.

The word "Adi" is more representative of "first" and "nath/a" is a sect or group of people. So if we look at the idea, rather than the person, deity or figure, of Sri Adinatha, the text is trying to establish a founding figure with an extraordinary ability — the first of a kind to be able to manipulate energy and harness the mind as a result of physical control. Another way to look at it is that this practice brings about transformation of power and gives the practitioner the ability that is theirs alone. We are all one of a kind — unique in our manifestation while still holding universal connectivity.

The ability to create delight is within. Whether we believe in Shiva, Hinduism or the practice of yoga, it is conceptually worth noting that Adinatha (the first of a kind) to manipulate Sri (the pathways - energetic, mentally, emotionally) connected to all that is known and unknown. That this can be directed with full consciousness is really a testament to the notion of human involution - the personal evolution of an individual. The sentence is not only homage to one bettering themselves but,

WILLIAM DUPREY

in addition, becoming the best possible being and one full of their own power. This conquest for power or acceleration of a super human is not unknown in story, literature or humankind. However, it is here that I interpret the passage to be specific to yoga: that it is not by oppositions that we gain power and, further, that we do not need anything more — internal or external — other than taking that which is misaligned and balancing it as it is meant to be. We may even say that this particular balancing is yoga and that the aims by which we do the balancing — through the mind, body, work, knowledge, etc., — is the path in which we walk.

The inquiry itself is created. What does one desire to obtain? Why call Shiva? Why try to possess a state of yoga? The Pradipika answers that physical, hatha yoga, bodily mastery leads to raja yoga, mental mastery. Try to consider this: through that which is physical, is tangible, can be felt, we create steadiness, health of the body, direction into mental, conceptual, etherial weight (energy). Observe the mental weight that the world/life can place in our mind.

It is then understandable to see that the body is attended to through physical exercise and position which place stress on the physical systems and in turn affect the energetic systems. Therefore asana - physical exercise and manipulation - is the first step. Through asana, "steadiness, lightness, etc.," gained.

4. Masters. Siddhas

"These Mahasiddhas breaking the scepter of death, are roaming the Universe."

Masters or Mahasiddha are a way to trace lineage, order and the history of teachings.

I love this passage - roaming about in the universe - in that there are parts of us that continue on. I believe, in western culture, that there can be a tendency to glorify external things over internal value, and this perpetuates our cultural illnesses of acquiring versus having a grand internal experience. Similarly, senses are talked about in the yogic tradition as the ways in which we perceive that which is not of a particular value — such as postures having a particular look, and practices being right when done by said method.

A heavy asana culture exists in the global yoga community that has stretched far beyond the west. It is common to take the physical practice in one form that moves along the breath and instead see acrobatic transitions as achievement. It may surprise yoga practitioners that there are yogis, considered great hatha yogis, who rarely show or practice asana as they have now moved from physical to mental mastery, (raja yoga), and the asana comes into form while seated,-steadily in pranayama or meditation.

Who are these great contemplators? Svatmarama, writing the Hatha Yoga Pradipika, establishes that these masters, or maha siddhas, have conquered a quality which seems to put a limitation on expanding into involution. In this scenario, time is the limitation as time leads to death. Are we lead to believe that these masters, siddhas, yogis, could overcome death? Some traditions would say exactly that!

If we all keep living and dying, then it is important to really examine what is life and what is death. Dying can be something — anything — that stops us from fully living. Fully living is when we are involved fully in the purpose which we have in living.

When we start to add yogic thought, enters the pairs of opposites which come in the reflection of consciousness or in nature.

WILLIAM DUPREY

Nature is seen as reflection or illusion due to the subject of time and change. Whereas, consciousness is seen as complete, pure and without time. Though the Pradipika is not presenting thousand of years of scriptural writing and philosophy, inevitably there are traces of those thought constructs woven into the text. Chiefly the concept of duality where we see the pairs of opposites the world offers; the biggest being conscious energy and natural energy.

Similar to how we approach a new subject or point of view, we look at new things with memory, intellectual and experiential knowledge and a good amount of learned belief systems. Although, having established living as involved and purposeful and death as the ceasing of living, we immediately see some limitations when we apply that to the broader system of "I am alive or dead". These limitations may not be life changing ones, but they do ask the questions: Am I living with purpose? What is creating death in my living?

We age daily; this is not drastic. We reflect on last month, or a few years ago, when we were a specific age and recall the things we used to do. There is a death — desired or faded — from lack of use or a new habit that range from friendships to hobbies to exercise to pleasures. They are all subject to time. Some we select to let go of, some deaths we actually claim, and then there is the living with purpose. The intention of living purposefully is not to imply that you currently live without purpose or that you are lacking. We often think in left and right rather than center — or even better balance and riding that balance through all the peaks and valleys, the living and dying.

A general yoga perspective calls upon the idea of soul consciousness and, specifically, a witness within. Not only are we soul material, but we can witness this creation. The soul consciousness is also tied into the body. This would include the other bodies of energy associated with the physical body — the energetic, mental emotional, intellectual and blissful bodies (koshas). Think of these bodies as vehicles through which we experience. They can be tied to the overall experience, including the way in which we can witness our own consciousness. In fact, these bodies are what we refer to when we speak of karma. Though action is part of karma, it is not the sum total. The action we can produce is based on the body which we inhabit, and you may have noticed that we inhabit them differently. The difference is not only physical, mental, emotional, and spiritual. There is a natural maturation for us as we move through living. Some of our living is paired with suffering, based on our identity to things, outside of our purpose. In essence, we are incredibly tied to many threads of existence, and that existence is in all of us no matter how it is tied to another or outside of us.

These great masters were able to completely sever the threads that pulled them back into the limitations of the body. This is what we are referring to when we use the word unattached. The very action forms the basis for karma yoga — doing without the desire of reward. Hathavidya, the knowledge of hatha yoga, takes the first approach in manipulation of the physical. Steadiness can be made on a physical level, then it can be transferred or moved into the more energetic and mental, psychic bodies using aspects the techniques of yoga. Try not to immediately jump to power or controlling life and death, but instead think of controlling living with purpose and taming lost moments in living and now you are roaming through the universe without condition. In turn, our desire to seek happiness or avoid pain will be quieted as we create perfection through contentment.

5.   Three Tapas

"Like a house protects one from the heat of the Sun, Hatha Yoga protects its practitioner from the burning heat of the three types of pain; and, similarly, it is like the tortoise supporting, as it were, for those who are constantly devoted to the practice of Yoga."

Earlier, we discussed karma, the layers of sensation determined by the sheath through which we are experiencing those sensations, and yoga as a process through which we can learn to perceive with more accuracy. This accuracy or clarity is based on our own conscious trajectory and involutionary awareness which is changing with responsiveness to the world around and within us.

Conceptually, we may have this dialed in with accuracy. We can even understand how we perceive through the senses versus witness from the self, then responsibly create and adjust that which fills our own purpose and unlimited living. Perfection can have limitation as much as movement has exhaustion. Internally, for some, there is constant peace and contentment until they are interactive with the world. The best intention met with all the right motives and filled with absolute balance can be misperceived. Things may pass or change as we identify heavily on skills, occupation or partnership; as that change occurs, the role and relation is altered. Parenting lends a hand to the development of the child in a way where you have to adjust rules and norms along the way. You yourself might have reflected that your own motto has changed when tested.

There are many factors that are completely out of your control, and they can have the same strong effect on you as if they come directly from you. Astrology examines the influence of planets on the individual depending on time and location of birth. Certain parts of the world can see astronomical phenomena depending on location and yet, even though the same phenomena is happening elsewhere, it may not be visible. Still, it exists and may be felt. Similarly, astrology and astronomy are measuring the influence of energy like shadows cast in absence of sun. The measurement of that energy, or lack of it, is codified in astrology and is appeased by gemology, ayurveda, mantra and yoga practices which appease some of the potential malefic effects on your system as it matures into life.

Life has a variety of energies. Planetary alignment and time are also aspects that can aid or pose limitation on our understanding and perception. Whatever the influences, living involves suffering and death with a myriad of shades all the way from start to finish and over again. The Pradipika highlights the external notions in things that can temper, heat or place fire in our physical, mental and emotional, or spiritual states of understanding and awareness. That rather quickly these practices build a house of energy around the practitioner to protect from these external and internal influences.

When the three tapas are in control, there is potential for body mind spirit harmony and therefore a place for the state of yoga. The physical and energetic practices temper the body, mind and breath to lift toward spirit. Tapas is to temper, burn, or heat, and this causes the separation of that which is not spirit from all things that try to appear as such.

WILLIAM DUPREY

6.   Room. Time. Country

"Having seated in such a room and free from all anxieties, he should practice Yoga continuously, as instructed by his Guru."

Proper protocol and provisions are established for the success of the student. Presently, we may find it overwhelmingly difficult to be in a well governed place — especially in rise of global and local issues. When we are in the face of heightened challenges with social issues and while we may desire positive change or advancements in ideology of thought to suit our modern life, which can be so frustrating we seek refuge in a like-minded community or isolation. Membership in a monastery or retreating into nowhere may not be a modern solution either as we tend to see isolation as self ostracizing or punishment from an interpersonal lens.

These classical settings were established as a way where one could live on alms and free from obstacles that came about in a societal position. We have to look at the isolation factor. This was not a way to escape from society but served as a form of purification in thought. Established steadiness in a place without obstacles and anxieties was a key to success. It is easy to say that this is simple and anyone can do it, yet we cannot even take a break from our mobile devices longer than a day. This is not to say that a yogi is limited to living in isolation, but that isolation was a classical preparation where yogis would establish practices which were given by the guru.

Modern life does not allow us to retreat so readily. Dharma Mittra, my first guru, once said, "If you can meditate in a busy city, you can meditate anywhere." I believe there is truth to this; however, I am not shunning isolation either. If one does live alone in practice, it is advisable to have a guru to instruct them how. Even an occasional visit allows for monitoring the progress of the student. The guru is there to assist the student and initiate them into right knowledge.

Rather than living in a small apartment in the middle of a city or alone in the wilderness, find a place, a seat (or asana) and think of the qualities of your guru or someone you revere. See your energy become more and more optimal, evolved, advancing. The key here is to remove the anxieties of your mind and all a proper hermitage for the experiences of your practices. Change is allowing that which is perfect and complete within to radiate through every aspect of you. That is success.

7. Success & Secrets

"To be able to practice yoga, one must possess enthusiasm, zeal, courage, and a firm faith in tattvajnana [philosophical knowledge]. One should also not mingle with the crowd. With these qualities, an aspirant can attain yoga."

Jois, Sri K. Pattabhi. Yoga Mala: The Seminal Treatise and Guide from the Living Master of Ashtanga Yoga (Kindle Locations 1955–1964). Farrar, Straus and Giroux. Kindle Edition.

"A Yogin desirous of Siddhi should keep the knowledge of Hatha Yoga secret; for it becomes potent by concealing, and impotent if revealed." Pacham Singh

I have selected two passages here which are incredibly impactful, outlining methods of success for the practitioner. Together these make some of the most perfect passages on the theory of yoga.

Notice the translation above mentions eager enjoyment, confidence, determination, sincerity, conviction, and being self reflective as method to establish, obtain yoga. Yoga is a doctrine of habit thus through it we become attached. It is common to feel in a yoga community a rather large and loose concept on non-attachment. Often the very word 'attachment' is talked about like a fear or pandemic and indicates a preference for a non-emotional, non-feeling state. However, those of you that have a regular practice know from experience that, in order for a result to occur, we have to attach ourselves to our practice. Further, we know that in making a habit, we can create a pattern for the mind to work in-safety – sometimes it is safe to stay in the familiar even if that is not to our own personal evolution.

When we turn to the Pradipika on asana alone, Swatmarama states that it is the first accessory of yoga — meaning it should be attended to first and that through asana we gain steadiness, lightness and health.

It is common for us to translate asana as a physical posture. Certainly, when we look at or show an asana, it is easy to see the muscles moved in a particular way or stance. Much of popular culture — inside and out of yoga communities — place a huge emphasis on the practice of asana. We naturally deduce that yoga therefore is asana.

In classic yogic literature, the word asana is often translated as a "seat." We can expand on the idea of a physical stance to understand that asana is more of a position that we take on as a seat in life.

It is very much a part of the practice, no matter the path of yoga, to steady that which is unsteady — to form a position in which we can remain with a conviction that is not full of rigidity. Gratification of the immediate creates the ability for the practitioner to know steadiness amidst the altering world around us. This state facilitates even-minded apprehension and coming into a suspended state of thought where thought comes at the mind like a sieve and a selection is chosen to be occupied by the mind as opposed to the mind being overwhelmed.

I believe this is why words such as "enthusiasm, boldness, firmness, discrimination of truth, conviction, and the avoidance of public gatherings" are chosen carefully to really bring to attention that control of the senses and distraction are not a small feat.

It also does something interesting in keeping it secret.

8. 11 Asanas. Plus 4

"Being the first accessory of Hatha Yoga, Asana, is steady posture, health and lightness of body. I am going to describe certain Asaans which been adopted by Munis like Vasishtha, etc., and Yogis like Matsyendra, etc."

The above passage creates validity in the process while showing the lineage or tradition of imparting knowledge from one teacher to another (maintaining an origin and order). It also subtly hints at the idea that one can obtain success from the potency of the practice although it does take a lot of time. Think of a muni like a holy person of holy persons (in term of order, muni would be high up on spiritual attainment) who often lives in isolation and does not necessarily impart knowledge. The idea that they do not necessarily impart knowledge is of particular interest. The first guru I sat with taught that truly learning a technique was to a know a technique and to really know it takes a couple of years. Being able to teach a technique means taking time with that technique, (in this example two years), then proceeding to to teach it. Yoga is holistic in practice — which is to say that everything comes to the surface when we practice. With the physical comes the emotional, mental and energetic, and spiritual. However, the results tend to be predominantly related to the task at hand (i.e. physical gives physical results and energetic gives energetic ones). I say this not to be obvious but to add a level of transparency to the practice. When we manipulate any system, that system is affected thus when we experiment with said system, it will bring a result to that system. We do not know how long it will take for the result to occur within the system. The result is an alteration, rise, shift in the system being manipulated. This is why many books of yoga will talk casually about asana but will give a strong warning when it comes to pranayama and other energy related practices. As mentioned, waiting a couple of years to understand more energetic practices through experience is ideal before sharing or teaching others as you cannot determine the rate of growth from the practice per individual.

To a certain degree, we start with asana first because much of it has already been established and the practice of asana creates steadiness, health and lightness. Asana asks us to peer into systems of health, such as ayurveda and the dhatus (tissues of energy). As the postures are explained within the Pradipika, they are not attributed to having benefits pertaining to a lot of the musculature of the system. Instead — and more on par with the classical methodology of hatha yoga — an array of benefits are expressed that gravitate toward: removing all diseases, increasing appetite and agni (gastric fire), destroying poison, balancing the dhatus (tissues of energy specifically categorized as bile, phlegm, and wind), raising kundalini and removing fatigue. Diseases are not classified and muscles are not mentioned. The postures express great benefits, However, when you look underneath, they are balancing the source of the energy at the first level; that is to say, the postures are directing prana through the most accessible paths. Some of these paths relate to the journey of kundalini, but most are working on creating extensive energy through the system in preparation for what is to come.

Though we may look at these grouping of poses as preparatory, there no instructions on how they are to be done and for how long. There is no mention of a particular breathing technique. There are no drishtis (points to focus on with your eyesight) mentioned. Outside of instruction of the posture, which tends to have to be deciphered, the benefits are categorized as mentioned.

WILLIAM DUPREY

This is exactly what is intriguing. Modern texts offer benefits based on anatomical results that are mostly physically related. At times, you will see texts addressing circulatory, respiratory and occasionally endocrine systems. The Hatha Yoga Pradipika focuses on the energy within that can steer the body toward a peak state of experience (kundalini and, in turn, samadhi) rather than physical ability. In this way, we start to see that the postures represent the vessel (physical body) and one is manipulating the postures through a technique or tool. It is unclear what that technique or tool is; however, indication is made repeatedly that the postures are balancing the physical and energetic systems.

During extensive practices with these postures, a type of compounding and transmutation in the process was revealed to me. Yes, the postures could be performed in order, but if you connected your concentration throughout, it could be carried from posture to posture. Choosing a constant pranayama (initially ujjayi) and an internal drishti, there seemed to be places in which energy and mental concentration gravitated toward in each posture. Doing them in the listed order brought about a particular experience that lead to timed practice (postures held for five minutes and upwards) and shifting concentrations in techniques. In time, the postures stopped being a sequence and became eleven opportunities toward the same peak experience. If you will, imagine each posture as a road. Each road leads to a gate. It does not matter which road you take, they all lead to the gate. Once you reach the gate, there is no need for the other postures. Mentally, the practice widened from being about accumulation and turned into allowing and creating an opportune environment — getting things aligned from the concentration and breath.

The experiences in the asana became a gateway to understanding more in asana. I have seen many students also experience similar results. However, it is important to remember that asana is practiced for steadiness, health and lightness.

"Śiva taught 84 Asanas. Of these the first four being essential ones."

Following the eleven postures, the text draws your attention back to Śiva and those asana most essential to the practice. The text does not list the 84 asanas. The additional four (4) mentioned are contemplative in nature and manipulate the

WILLIAM DUPREY

energetics systems (koshas, nadis, etc,.) directly. There is often the use of bandha and kumbhaka with particular drishtis to create a mudra from the body. The heavy details emphasizing the indispensable four seats should not be left out. Rather than detail them with illustration, particularly because they are not preliminary, I have chosen to detail experiences from their practice in lieu of providing a visual or suggested way to practice them. Overall, they are not complicated in performance. There are stages to some of the postures and suggested times of practice (i.e. 12 years) or notion of dietary measures as an accelrator of siddha (perfection).

9. Nada

"There is no Asana like the Siddhasana and no Kumbhaka like the Kevala. There is no Mudra like the Khechari and no Laya like the Nada (Anahata Nada)."

One of the the most spectacular truths revealed is that yoga — or the application of a yoga technique — eventually leads to the knowledge of the technique or of yoga as a state or condition that it is void of the method used. You know the technique and knowing it means understanding, by immersing in the state it produces. That product is yoga.

The concept of 'to strike' or 'pierce' as being an integral part of Hatha Yoga — and not necessarily the combination of opposites, often depicted as the joining of the sun or moon or female and male energy — is often overlooked in modern views on yoga. This misunderstanding is so deep in yoga communities that we often see men as tied to Shiva, Brahma, etc., and women as tied to Shakti, Durga, etc., rather than seeing the culmination of both energies into something that is now and living within all beings. That piercing, or breaking, comes not as violence or aggression but the ability to obtain the essence of the self.

Self awareness requires distinct methodology in the beginning. Application of technique is what we first learn. This application brings about steadiness and lightness in the body. The internal energy becomes even. The mind becomes even. We discontinue identifying with the opposites that pull the mind and energy out of this metabolic balance — a balance around which the world seems to spin with fluctuation and yet we remain able to adapt and move while internally we are steady in our own clarity. This requires a piercing or striking of the qualities with which we have identified as the self as well as the cause of discomfort, suffering or pleasure. Let me clarify that this is not becoming apathetic or being able to move through an array of emotions, but rather it is learning how and what the self looks like individually and in each occurrence.

Through the use of opposites, we understand the shelf life of emotions and living. There is a termination point and, therefore, the experience is complete and real and felt, but it is also temporary to the seeker of individual spirit. What was once used to measure the experience or to pierce the illusion surrounding it is no longer of importance. Technique becomes useless at this point as for the yogini. Life has revealed a purpose within.

It is kind to note the beginning stages of this process as subtle experiences of balancing between the spiritual world and everyday living. Personally, this was one of my initial inquiries into offering a traditional and practical approach in a training program. Often, practitioners will be in a juxtaposition between life and sadhana (yoga practices) — as if they are in a constant struggle which is often an alarming place to be. It can feel as though the alliances they have in life are less flavorful than they once believed, or they may see these alliances with more clarity. That luster lost in intimate relationships can be heart challenging for some and freeing for others. When we move more into the self, we often learn how to care more deeply for our own growth and needs, so this is an excellent time to use a new tool to communicate the growth, evolvement and involvement of this new life — going beyond the shell and directly into the essence of you. This is beyond application, beyond sound, beyond movement, beyond breath.

WILLIAM DUPREY

The practitioner has an incredible journey ahead of them through the path of detachment, to the attachment to techniques, to allowing the essence of self within. In the end, we are left with absolutely nothing and everything riding side by side, stretched out forever.

10. Food

"Abstemious feeding is that in which 3/4 of hunger is satisfied with food, well cooked with ghee and sweets, and eaten after offering it to Śiva."

Food has become a dirty word in modern yoga communities. The type of food you eat has become a criteria of what a yogi actually is. In essence, we look more to what one should eat to be a yogini instead of at what one does. Outside of a temporary diet used during the initial stages of asana and pranayama, the diet is mostly met with moderation rather than prescribing the content. We have heard a lot of recent practitioners of yoga urge the vegetarian and vegan agendas for eating. A vegetarian diet certainly has benefits on the planet, but sustainability is another topic. Alternatively, there is the argument that vegan eating helps lessen the karmic burden one may encounter in life. However, the body is also tied to karma. Now look at karma as a sheath that is wrapped around multiple layers of the essence of the soul. The body is a sheath wrapped around all the energy you understand and that which you are trying to understand. Some of your desire for self-awareness is motivated by perception, desire for pleasure, aversion to suffering, time, contentment, cleanliness and truth. Therefore, the body is of great importance as it houses all of the energy systems, and the gooey center is the soul which is expressed to be the size of one's own thumbprint residing in the center of your chest. [1]

Karma being the body is also tied to our physical existence; without a body, we would not be living as we are now, reading these words, thinking, breathing. Peering deeper into this relationship with karma (the body) and realization (consciousness or even godliness), it is a wonder we struggle with that which is tied to the body (physical) and that which is not (metaphysical)? The construct of proof (seeing, feeling tangible results, knowing) and the conceptual (change within idealized thought; a type of metabolic state) are so difficult to put into balance. There many theories amongst many paths of spirituality and religion. While they may argue individual

---

[1] "That thumb-sized being enshrined in the heart,
Ruler of time, past and future,
To see whom is to go beyond all fear,
Is the Self indeed. For this Self is supreme!"

Excerpt From: Eknath Easwaran. "The Upanishads." iBooks. Part 2, Section 1, Verse 12

aspects, they agree in other areas. This can feel like a giant tug-o-war on the mind, body and spirit.

Diet, by definition, is food and drink consumed habitually or to benefit the individual thus gauging when more or less is required. That gauge is moderation. Moderation is creating change based on pure needs and to suit the rhythms of the body (exercise, age, health), the mind (psychological states and perceptions) and spiritual (faith in the internal and external). Through moderation, we learn not only what is required when it comes to food and drink but what the body requires to suit the physical and spiritual paradigm in this current existence.

The passage above suggest a particular moderation. That of the stomach being 1/4 (one quarter) empty for the expansion that occurs. The contents of the stomach are 3/4 water and food (in equal measure) and 1/4 air. As part of the act of eating, a portion of your meal is offered to Siva. I have heard stories of gurus who were so full of prana that when they cooked, the sishya (student) would be so full off of very little food as it was abundant with energy (prana).

Prana is more difficult to transmit on such a level; however, it is expanded upon quite easily on physical levels. Prana is often translated as 'energy' or 'life force' but it is more directly translated as 'first or most basic unit of measured energy.' I often use this definition to indicate that prana can be felt — meaning that you become aware of feeling your energy change.

One way prana works on the system is through clean food and water. Other methods are exposure to nature, being around others who are like minded or inspirational, and hearing satsangs (discussions on consciousness). Pranayama — which is often called breathing techniques — has a lot less to do with breathing and a lot more to do with how we extend our relationship with prana. Eventually, it comes under the control of the mind as willpower.

Food starts us off on the prana journey. Moderation and pleasantries allow us joy and ease as well as the ability to use our energy easily and at will.

11. Societal Position

"Whether young, old or too old, sick or lean, one who discards laziness, gets success if he practices Yoga."

Some things are simple, inspirational and pointed at truth. Success is success and it knows no age. I will also add that our culture tends to place an importance on those who can perform postures rather than using postures for those who have not yet learned them. If we really want to make a yoga practice universal we will collectively focus more on populations (sick, weak, old, impoverished, etc.) that could benefit from yoga. In particular, asanas do not have to be complicated in order for them to be beneficial. Learning classical suryanamaskara (sun salutation) is all one needs. The postures represented in this book are specific to building a peak experience which is sometimes called shakti or raising kundalini. This achievement is for the benefit of all and all can benefit from it. I am not saying yoga is for everyone — not in the way most of us know and see it — but it can be, when we aim at allowing that which is within to expand to full potential in our right and light.

12. Success

"Success cannot be attained by adopting a particular dress. It cannot be gained by telling tales. Practice alone is the means to success. This is true, there is no doubt about it."

Cut to the cloth! While wearing a garment may show your interest in a subject, wearing it in shows your use and potential skill through repetition. A Persian rug increases value as it is walked on. Your feet, treading on the carpet, bring out all the dyes, colors become more vibrant and the value of the rug increases. The luster is lost if you roll it up and store it.

Yoga is an ideology of habit. Through repetition a luster is established. And only through the practice alone can a state of yoga be kept. Once you remove the cloth, the yoga should still be present. The knowledge that is attained — here, it is referred to as siddha or perfection — becomes contained within.

Asanas are postures. Kumbhaka refers to a pot or vessel and, within yoga, it is usually involves retaining the breath in or holding the breath out. Asana is designed for steadiness and lightness of the body. Health is said to be established by asana.

Asana is a means to cultivate prana or energy – to bring out the vibrancy of color in our rug analogy. Kumbhaka would be a way or inhabiting that in life. When we retain energy, we hold prana. Prana is the intelligence of which the universe is made.

By means of asana and kumbhaka, we cultivate the joys of life within and that seeps through attire or position.

13. Asanas

Sit in a space where you are free from all distractions. Make your space, even if it is temporary, delightful and enjoyable to be in.

Before you begin, place your energy awareness in your breathing and close your eyes. Try to develop a relationship exclusively with the breathing. It is continuous and may be uneven. Allow it to be as it is. As you connect with it, focus on the quality and clarity of the breath coming in and the breath going out. The in and out breath both make up one breath. Try to get the overall quality of the breath to be smooth and even, silent, inaudible to you. Visualize the breath as your energy filling and emptying everything. Visualize the energy expanding across your skin. Do this until you feel like you can keep returning to this breath/ energy connection. Let your mind follow the expansion on inhalation and integration on exhalation.

In the beginning, you will be thumbing though the following images to following images to see what each pose look like and how to practice it. In time, you will be able to go from pose to pose with your eyes closed the whole time. The descriptions below will include times when you should change your internal focus or how to direct the breath when it alters from the above exercise.

Svastikasana (fig. 1) is practiced by sitting with legs crossed and placing the tip of your right toes behind the back of your left knee and your left toes behind your right knee. Sit steady and observe your breathing.

Gomukhasana (fig. 2a) is practiced by crossing the right leg over the left. Place also the right arm behind head, left arm turned inward behind back. Hands may or may not reach behind the back. Place your breath attention on your shoulders or the right side of the body.

After some time, do the posture with the left leg over the right and the arms reversed (fig. 2b). The breath attention is on the shoulders or the left side of the body. Your arms may lose circulation while in this posture.

Virasana (fig. 3) is practiced by placing your left leg in what is commonly practiced as virasana. Place your right leg on top of your left leg in padmasana. Hands are in prayer, resting lightly on the head, fingers upward, elbows open. Focus on your breath as a long line from your seat though your spine to your fingertips. This posture is performed only on one side.

WILLIAM DUPREY

Kurmasana (fig. 4a) is practiced by placing arms behind bent knees, legs straight in front of you. Stretch the arms out as you hug your thighs toward your body to straighten your legs. The text refers to a cross legged variation (fig. 4b). Practice both variations with breath awareness on the sacrum and abdomen.

Kukkutasana (fig. 5) is practiced by sitting in padamasana and placing arms through the legs to lift the body up. Breath attention is on the entire body.

WILLIAM DUPREY

Uttanakurmasana (fig. 6) after kukkutasana, keep arms through legs, lay on your back, lift your head and reach your hands to clasp your fingers behind your neck. Your hands may barely move at first. Breath awareness is on the entire body and moves to kurma nadi (below your throat, above your sternum).

Dhanurasana (fig. 7) is practiced laying on the stomach, clasping feet and pulling them toward the shoulders. Breath awareness on the tip of the top to roof of the mouth.

Matsyendrasana (fig. 8a) is practiced seated, right leg over left,

twisting the trunk right and using the back of your left arm like

a lever to lift spine. Breath awareness is on the entire body. Both

directions are practiced (fig. 8b).

This posture is repeatedly listed in groups of essential postures as are the next three postures.

Paschimottanasana (fig. 9) is practiced seated with legs stretched out in a seated forward fold. Place your breath energy in your spine.

Mayurasana (fig. 10) is practiced by lifting the body off the floor. The hands are together and facing back with the elbows into the navel. This posture can be uncomfortable at first. Continue to practice it daily with breath attention on the whole body.

Shavasana (fig. 11) is practiced laying down. The breath control completely drops and all energy rests in the center of the chest. Practice for 10 minutes or longer.

WILLIAM DUPREY

At the conclusion of practice, sit and observe your energy in the same way you started the practice. Observation is key to experiential knowledge. If you enjoy further contemplation, read a few passages from 12. Light on Hatha Yoga and meditate on the meaning. This can be done alone or in conjunction with the physical practice. The poetic translation can be used in teaching classrooms, workshops, retreats or training programs. It can be used in practice or in comparison to the original text for deeper study. Paired with the physical practices, you will join experiential and contemplative energies together, with this there is no doubt toward your personal success in the practice.

Thank you for allowing me to share.

Follow this link for the complete guided practice with an additional relaxation technique:

https://vimeo.com/willduprey/lightonhathayoga

Glossary

Shri - classically a title of one who possess the ability to manipulate shakti; more commonly used as a title of reverence.

Adinatha - another name for Shiva.

Anahata Nada - often translated as sound of the heart and the sound heard there is a non sound, described as two objects that almost strike each other.

Asana - a posture or seat in classical hatha yoga, sometimes written yogasana.

Ashtanga - also written ashtangayoga; refers to the eight-limb (ashta-anga) path of yoga as written by Sage Patanjali; known as a method of yoga founded by K. Pattabhi Jois.

Atma - the soul both grand (paramatma) and individual (jivatma) are one in the same; realization in part is direct identity with the soul.

Bandha - often referred to as locks (or to stop) rather than as a lock (e.g. Panama Canal) that stores and delivers energy to different parts of the physical and energetic systems; physical and energetic activities used to capture the energy of the chakras; most notable are jalandhara bandha, uddiyana bandha and mula bandha which when combine become maha bandha — there are many more bandhas.

Brahma - God; often associated with being the first, one with out subject to any rules as show the purity and completeness of this being; also tied to the concept or idea or form.

Dharma - virtue, duty, law, purpose are a few of the many translations. Dharma is part of a larger system of thought in Sanatana Dharma and many eastern religions and philosophies. Dharma is part of the Purusharathas.

Dhatus - tissue and structures of the body from Ayurveda though referenced in texts on yoga; each tissue has a function.

Drishti - initial stage of concentration and pratyahara.

Durga - Goddess warrior associated with dharma and prosperity; consort of Shiva; seen sometimes as an incarnation of Pavarti.

Hatha - short for Hatha Yoga, also written as hathayoga or hathaviyda; a branch of yoga; meaning to strike or force; bodily mastery; Hathavidya refers more to the knowledge of hatha which could in turn mean Raja Yoga, referring to the whole branch of yoga which hatha falls under.

Hatha Yoga Pradipika - casually referred to as the Pradipika; sometimes written Hathayogapradipika; a text complied in the 15th Century by Yogi Svatmarama.

Hathavidya - see Hatha; the knowledge of hatha yoga; a collective school of thought founded by author and yoga educator, Will Duprey.

Karma - action; deed; the physical bodies (koshas) that surround the soul (atma); karma is strongly tied to ideas of rebirth (samsara) and samskara (mental impressions that continue to play a role in life lessons and perception).

Khechari - a specific mudra performed with the tongue and eyes. Koshas - sheaths; five (5) bodies that cover the soul each made up from different energies ranging from element based to knowledge.

Krama - see Vinyasa.

Kriya - action; often interchanged with the word 'karma;' a physical repletion (sometimes in conjunction with a visual process) used for purification and cleansing on energetic (and physical) parameters; a series of cleansing techniques performed before the practice of asana or at the time of physical and energetic disharmony that can lead to disease; a system taught by Sage Patanjali within the Yoga Sutras; a system taught by Pramahansa Yogananda.

Kundalini - a dormant form of shakti that is situated at the base of spine in the analogy of a serpent ready to rise; kundalini is made active (shakti) through practices of yoga and also by other methods.

Laya - Laya Yoga is based in Shakti and Tantra lineages and is later called Kundalini Yoga; considered one of four paths of yoga in the Shiva Samhita.

Mahasiddha - a siddha amongst siddhas.

Mantra - or mantram, refers to the mind though commonly thought of as chanting; a group of organized sound that bring about energetic and mental changes; a method of pranayama and invoicing a meditative transcendence or samadhi.

Mudra - a gesture often seen with hand placement used in a particular way to draw a quality, usually energetic, from macrocosm to microcosm; the gesture can be with hands, feet, body, eyes.

Munis - holy person who lives in isolation or silence and tends to be realized through experiential means rather than scriptural reference.

Nada - sound as a method of obtaining yoga; see anahata nada.

Nyaya - one of the six (6) schools of thought based in the Vedas with a strong emphasis on logic and knowledge.

Patanjali - a sage who most notably complied the Yoga Sutras with two distinct systems; kriya yoga and the eight limbed path.

Pradipika - short for Hatha Yoga Pradipika

Pranayama - prana is the most basic unit of measured energy often translated as life force or vital energy; ayama is to lengthen or extend; together this would indicated the lengthening or extension of life energy.

Pratyahara - a method for redirecting the energy of the senses toward dharana or concentration.

Raja - king or royal; short for Raja Yoga, a branch of yoga referring to mental mastery or control; referring to ashtanga yoga system or Patanjali.

Sadhana - a method to obtain truth; a practice within yoga aimed at self realization.

Samadhi - a state of experience met through meditation; there are different levels of samadhi or absorption which can last from moments to indefinite.

Samhita - a grouping, layering of texts in the Vedas; can be translated as unified or joined together.

Sankhya - one of the six (6) schools of thought based in the Vedas with a strong emphasis on duality; Yoga largely follows Sankya but implements practice and samadhi; also written Samkhya.

Sat - truth or true related to unchangeable; a prefix for good or virtuous.

Shakti - divine energy often seen in the feminine form entangled with Shiva; an active form of kundalini; innate power brought about in human beings through spiritual and personal transformation that may or may not lead to consciousness.

Shankara - formal name Adi Shankara; philosopher accredited to Advaita Vedanta and the ananda monastic order; most notably for commentary on Brahma Sutras.

Shiva - God; the first yogi; seen as a derivative of Rudra; Shiva often holds the energy of transformation or dissolution and is the principle deity of workshop in tantra and siddha lineages.

Siddha - perfection, or one who has reached a perfected state.

Sutras - short for Yoga Sutras of Patanjali; there are many other sutras.

Svatmarama - a yogic sage most notable for compiling The Hatha Yoga Pradipika.

Tantra - to weave, loom or stretch across; a methodology or application that exists in many branches of logic in Hinduism, Buddhism and without religion; esoteric and ritualistic.

Tapas - the root 'tap' is to burn; we can view tapas as a way to temper, produce heat which in turn creates transformation, in that regard, the transformation is not only physical but includes mental and spiritual changes.

Tarka - contemplation or reflection; originally part of the shadanga, or six-limbed system of yoga.

Ujjayi - a technique used in the breathing methodology component of pranayama.

Vinyasa - short for Vinyasa Krama or Vinyasakrama; method of Hatha Yoga as popularized through the teaching of Tirumalai Krishnamacharya — his most notable students being: Indra Devi, K. Pattabhi Jois, B. K. S. Iyengar, T. K. V. Desikachar, Srivatasa Ramaswami and A. G. Mohan.

Yoga - a school of logic based on Sankhya; a state in which one can enter by methodologies outlined in the various paths to yoga; to unify, yoke or tied together.

Yoga Sutras - refers to Yoga Sutras of Patanjali; classically called yoga aphorisms, more commonly called Sutras or ashtanga yoga; a text synthesizing yoga traditions written around 400 CE.

Notes and Quotes

1. Feuerstein, Georg (2013-09-11). The Yoga Tradition: It's History, Literature, Philosophy and Practice (Kindle Locations 7580-7582). Hohm Press. Kindle Edition.

2-4. Jayashree, Dr. M. A. (2006). Hathayogapradipika, Anahata Research Foundation.

5. Jois, Sri K. (2010). Yoga Mala: The Original Teachings of Ashtanga Yoga, North Point Press: 2 edition.

6-10. Jayashree, Dr. M. A. (2006). Hathayogapradipika, Anahata Research Foundation.

11. Easwaran, Eknath (1987, 2007). The Upanishads, Katha Upanishad (p.79, verse 12-13), The Blue Mountain Center of Meditation.

12-13. Jayashree, Dr. M. A. (2006). Hathayogapradipika, Anahata Research Foundation.

14. Basu, Srichandra, B.A., F. T. S. (1887). The Esoteric Philosophy of The Tantras, The Shiva Sanhita, Calcutta Heeralal Dhole

References

Akers, Brian Dana. (2002). The Hatha Yoga Pradipika, YogaVidya.com.

Bühnemann, Gudrun. (2007). Eighty-four Asanas in Yoga: A Survey of Traditions, D. K. Printworld Pvt. Ltd.

Ganapathy, T. N. (2003). The Yoga of Siddha Boganathar, Kriya Yoga Publications.

Govindan, M. (1993). Thirumandiram: A Classic of Yoga and Tantra (Three Volume Set), Kirya Yoga Publications.

Jayashree, Dr. M. A. (2006). Hathayogapradipika, Anahata Research Foundation.

Muktibodhananda, Swami. (1998). Hatha Yoga Pradipika, Bihar School of Yoga; 3rd edition.

Pancham, Singh. (1819). The Hatha Yoga Pradipika, Dev Publishers.

Zvelebil, Kamil V. (1996). Siddha Quest for Immortality, Red Wheel/Weiser; UK ed.

Printed in the United States
by Baker & Taylor Publisher Services